T0131892

I Miss That Kiss

ROBERT ROGERS

To order additional copies of this book, contact:
Xlibris
844-714-8691
www.Xlibris.com
Orders@Xlibris.com

ISBN: 978-1-6698-7194-1 (sc)
ISBN: 978-1-6698-7195-8 (e)

Print information available on the last page

Rev. date: 03/23/2023

Contents

A Cowboy

I'm a Cowboy
Can't sing worth a dam
Struggle playing the guitar
Never look for a fight
Only fight for what's right
Treat women with regard
Shake hands with the men
The Cowboy hat has meaning
Shows what I am
I wear it with satisfaction
It invites attention
That belt is not an ornament

It secures those tight jeans
We all know what that means
Cowboy boots are suitable
Help confirm me
A Cowboy
The horse I no longer ride
Walk main street with pride
Wave to those who look my way
They may not know what to say
Just survey
Cowboys may not endure
Only memories will remain

A Hero

We all need a hero
You may not know
She is the one I love so
I do not know where to start
It will come firm my heart
I live on this island of darkness
I watch her with those three kids
Teaches them how to live
Tells me what is right
Whispers to me at night

She is my love light
It shines bright
She is my hero
I do not think she knows
I need to tell her so
She rescued me
Pulled me from life's despair
Revived my care
We all need a hero

A Miracle Day

It was a miracle day
I sat on the bench
Feeling rather low
The exact date I don't know
It was warm
The grass was green
She was the prettiest I had ever seen
Hair short and brown
A smile that glowed
A blouse cut low
A stunning site
She walked my way
I didn't know what to say
She sat beside me
Is this a dream?
A miracle that I see
My dream was with me
She must be real
I know how I feel
Not a word was said
She held my hand
It's not a dream
My heart beats fast
How long will this last
Miracles can come true

Candle

Love is like a candle
It glows when lit
Bums bright
Can be extinguished with a single breath
It may no longer spread light
A candle can be relit
Change that darkness into light
She came 1o me
Struck a feeling in me
Set my heat alight
It still bums
Her feelings have slowly changed

The candle flickers
Her love may not last
Fail to burn bright
Leave me in darkness
I can only hope that the wick will awaken
I want to hold my hands close
Feel the warmth
Touch her again
Let love purge the darkness
Love can last for a long time
Extinguished only when the darkness is endless

Despair

She sat on the couch
Quiet
Wanted something that might be
It was clear to me
It puzzled me
I asked
Is it something I might see
She gently looked at me
Why do you ask
I want to know
I do love you so
With a gentle nod
No, it's just me
I'm living with regret
I live in despair
My longing will not come true
It is not you
It's just me
I was once pretty
That will no longer be
Age has its old
I'm getting old
I smiled and said
Life has is faults
Nothing we can change
You are still pretty
You have to trust me
Others agree
Believe me
Believe us all

Don't Cry

Don't cry when I'm no longer with you
Don't shed tears on my grave
My life has been kind
I've loved you a long, long time
Just remember what we had
Loving feelings last
Remember the past
We walked together
Saw the sunshine bright
Loved the night
Held each other so very tight
Don't cry
You will be alright
I will always be with you
Remain deep in your heart
Even when we are apart
You will remember
Take that ring from your finger
Your thoughts should not linger
Learn to smile again
I will be with you
Smile
Don't cry

Don't Have to Tell Me

You don't have to tell me
I know you love me
I love you the way you are
I see it in your eyes
When you are with me
Your eyes glow bright
I realize I'm right
When you touch me
I know you love me
You don't need to tell me
I just know
In the night you hold me tight
Words are not needed
Your body tells me so
I'm never alone
Love is always with me
You do nothing wrong
It's just the way you are
Others may not know
I don't bother to tell them so
I just smile and hold your hand
Wait for the night
Hold you tight
Words are momentary
Love remains

Find Her

I need to find someone
I search for a woman
I sit in this house alone
Where do I start?
I really don't know
The internet is there
I am reluctant to share
The women I find really don't care
Only looking for fleeting events
Some only search for sexual intents
There is no tender care
Finding an affectionate woman seems rare
I don't know where to search

I just stay here alone
I'm not looking for a wife
A woman who cares
A companion
Enjoy having fun together
Share our laughs
Walk in an inspiring sunshine
We could enjoy a glass of wine
Have an engaging conversation during dinner
Go to a Garth Brooks concert
What could be finer?
Will I ever find her?

I Miss That Kiss

The World is moving too fast
Nothing seems to last
I remember that drive-in movie
The girls I once kissed
The speaker on the door
That doesn't exist anymore
I once called from a comer phone
It is gone
It's a technological race
A winged pace
Old times take flight
Never return
I once shifted the gears in that Chevy
It's no longer the same
This pace will never cease
Just increase
No one reads a book
Vinyl records have disappeared
They were replaced
Reel to reel tapes
Records
Compact disks
The iPhone has taken their place
What will tomorrow bring?
Nothing seems to last
I still miss that drive-in movie kiss

I Remember

She will never go back
I watched my mother pick that cotton
She pulled that long sack
She walked along that row
Why she did I still don't know
She wanted to clothe me and Nell
I remember it well
Her hands were strong
Often bleed
I asked her why
She never said
She just picked the cotton
Drug that long sack
The sun was hot
She never complained

She looked at me and said
I do it for you and Nell
I can't forget those words
I still remember what we had
A loving mother that cared
I still see those bleeding hands
The blood mixed with that white cotton
No one cared
Except me and Nell
Others watched as she pulled those bows
Drug that sack
I still remember
I hope other mothers never have to pick cotton
Red blood and white cotton should never mix
I remember it well

I'm Coming Home

I want to go back to when you
loved me
What use to be
I'm coming home
Please believe me
I don't want to be alone
I've made mistakes
I want to hold you again
Tell you how I feel

I want to be with you
Please believe me
Let me come back
I want it to be forever
I've changed
I'll knock on your door
Please open it
Believe what you see
It's a different me

Let me come in
See me again
I'm coming home
Loving you will never end
Love me again
Let me hold you
Show you how I feel
Know that my love is real
Forgive me

Phone Cry

I can hear the phone cry
It sounds like a long-distance call
It must be her
Searching for what she once knew
She said I'll try to forget this lonesome place
Travel somewhere new
Never again feel unwanted
She left without a word
Wanted to find something new
Try to forget this place
She said I want to escape this feeling
Find a new life
One without this lonesome strife
Feel wanted
I'm crazy for loving you
That phone began to cry
I now know why
It was the things I didn't do
I love her but seldom told her so
I should answer
Never again hear that phone cry
Tell her I love her
I can amend
I'm still in love with her
Cry with her

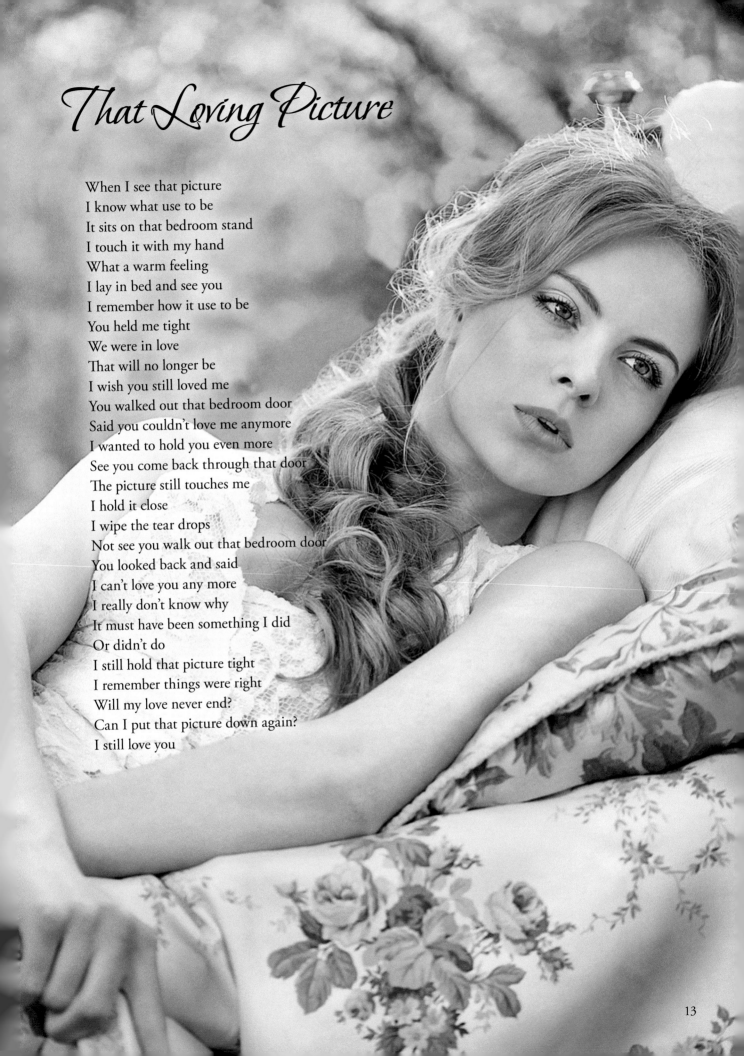

That Loving Picture

When I see that picture
I know what use to be
It sits on that bedroom stand
I touch it with my hand
What a warm feeling
I lay in bed and see you
I remember how it use to be
You held me tight
We were in love
That will no longer be
I wish you still loved me
You walked out that bedroom door
Said you couldn't love me anymore
I wanted to hold you even more
See you come back through that door
The picture still touches me
I hold it close
I wipe the tear drops
Not see you walk out that bedroom door
You looked back and said
I can't love you any more
I really don't know why
It must have been something I did
Or didn't do
I still hold that picture tight
I remember things were right
Will my love never end?
Can I put that picture down again?
I still love you

The Cadillac

She sent me a message
I do wonder why
Could it be a picture of me
Or that old Cadillac
I don't know
What should I do
Is it me she wants to see?
It must be the car
It's a star
It shines bright
Even in the night
An appealing sight
Ask her to meet me?

Take a ride with me?
I'm anxious to see
That car has been with me a long time
Like a woman
I treat her kind
Touch her gently
The lights shine bright
The engine is quiet
That back seat is soft and tight
Everything seems right
We shall see
When she meets me

The Mirror Tells The Truth

The mirror tells the truth
It bothers me
I don't like what I see
It's not me
I know how I feel
The mirror is real
It reflects a strange image
One I don't know
My reflection shows a different me
I think the mirror lies
My dark hair looks white
My bright eyes are unclear
I once liked what the minor shows

I concede
The image has changed
I must be getting old
I saw you step beside me
It seems you have the same feelings
Your red hair has streaks of grey
The reflections are real
Our images have change
It just doesn't feel right
Let's walk away
Forget what we see
There will always be a young you and me

Unknown Future

Life spins in unknown ways
It continues to change
We don't know what the future will bring
We can only guess
It changes with unknown events
We wade through life
We can't turn the tide
It simply washes over us
We struggle and breath deep
Hold our heads above the waves
Swim in life's rushing waters
Feel the cold and the warmth
Hope to survive
Stay alive
Time is like a distant bell that tolls
It's heard with doubt
We continue to search the future
Hoping we can find it
But life spins in unknown ways
It remains in futures swirling waters
It's hard to foretell
We can only hope for the best
Let the unknown future choose the rest

Wanting Love

She sent a picture
Jut for me
I found a woman that wants me
Something I did
Or something I said
I don't know why
I'm a lot older
It seems to matter not
She said she loved me
She must have lost her mind
She is a different kind
A woman with desire
Why so kind?
Will I make her mine?
Why choose me?
It's hard to believe

She just likes what she sees
I'm not a handsome man
I just do what I can
I asked her why
Waited for her reply
I want to hold her hand
See a gleam in her eyes
See her surprise
Why an older man?
It's hard to understand
It's her desire
I hear it in her voice
It's quite with a loving smile
I said we should wait awhile
A wanting love can be unknown
She just said she loves me

Who AM I

Who am I
It's a question I ask myself
I can't find the answer
I walk through this life
Remember the joys
Have those cloudy days
Is this the way it should be?
Is it meant to be this way?
I just can't say
I wish I know what I am
It's hard to understand
I search for the answer
Tread through each day
They blend
Every day seems the same
Am I to blame?
Why can't the joy last forever
Discount the cloudy days
I don't know the answer
Who am I
My life is mired in the question
I may never find the answer
Live with the joys and clouds
Battle through each day
Bear the search
Who am I?
I may never know

Wild Bill

I loved that wild Bill
I always will
He was wild as Hell
I remember him well
He looked at me with that wicked smile
I was intrigued
He said
We only live once
Let us be wild and free
Our love was unconstrained
I wish it remained
We traveled the country
Home was unknown
Drank the strangest wine
Ate in unexpected places
Watched the cotton grow
Swam in the Ocean water
Times were wild
Lasted for quite a while
But everything ends
We have gone separate ways
I still wish for those beguiling days

Robert Rogers is a retired Army officer. He spent 21 years in the US Army, completed two tours during the Vietnam War and was awarded a Silver Star for gallantry. He grew up in an impoverished environment in Oklahoma and California. He acquired a Master's degree in Speech and has written fiction and poem books. He resides a Leavenworth a small town in Kansas situated on the banks of the Missouri river.

Printed in the United States
by Baker & Taylor Publisher Services